☀ Summer ☀
BULLETIN
BOARDS
for Sunday School

Publisher ....*Arthur L. Miley*

Author ....*Carolyn Passig Jensen*

Art Director.......................................*Debbie Birch*

Cover Design ....*Gary Zupkas*

Production Director......................*Barbara Bucher*

Production Assistant ....*Valerie Fetrow*

Illustrator...*Fran Kizer*

Production Artist ....*Nelson Beltran*

Proofreader ....*Barbara Bucher*

Rainbow Books

Copyright © 1997 • Ninth Printing
Rainbow Books • P.O. Box 261129 • San Diego, CA 92196

#RB36194
ISBN 0-937282-36-7

CONTENTS

4

Introduction

Children learn best and remember more when they can see and visualize what they are taught. In fact, we learn 83 percent by sight and only 12 percent by hearing and touch together. But when hearing, touch *and* sight are combined, learning is much easier and effective.

Bulletin boards are a very effective way to teach children important biblical concepts so they will remember them. Because bulletin boards are colorful and attention-getting, children are naturally drawn to them and to the lessons they teach.

Today, bulletin boards are far more than simply boards to hold announcements and notices. Think of bulletin boards as an important part of your Sunday school or Bible classroom for several reasons:

- Bulletin boards are simple, inexpensive and colorful ways to decorate your classroom and provide an attractive learning environment
- Bulletin boards help children visualize and remember important spiritual concepts far longer than just talking about them
- Bulletin boards stimulate discussion and learning of Bible truths
- Bulletin boards help focus children's attention on important concepts you want to teach
- Bulletin boards help relate spiritual concepts to the children's everyday lives
- Bulletin boards motivate children to think critically and creatively
- Bulletin boards display useful information, announcements and invitations
- Bulletin boards provide an opportunity for children and teachers to relate to each other as they construct bulletin boards together

This book (and the other three books in this series) contain 13 seasonal Bible bulletin boards which can help you effectively teach biblical concepts in the ways listed above. The patterns and instructions in this book make it easy to construct delightful bulletin boards, and you won't need a lot of artistic talent to be successful!

Each bulletin board includes complete instructions and suggestions for borders, background, materials and how to put everything together. Full-size patterns are also provided, as are large headline letters and three seasonal borders and corners. All patterns, letters and borders may be used right out of the book or traced, enlarged, reduced, duplicated or photocopied to make attractive classroom bulletin boards.

Each bulletin board also includes a suggested Bible Memory Verse for the class to learn together and ideas for using the bulletin board to teach important spiritual concepts. (The King James Version of the Bible is used unless noted otherwise.)

Each bulletin board is designed for use in Sunday schools. Many may also be used in kids clubs, Vacation Bible School, children's church, Christian schools or anywhere the Bible is taught. The age of children for which the bulletin board is appropriate is also noted.

So . . . turn your classroom into an exciting learning environment with the colorful seasonal Bible-teaching bulletin boards in this book!

How to Create Beautiful Bulletin Boards Using the Materials in this Book

Each of the 13 Bible-teaching bulletin boards for Summer in this book contains complete instructions and full-size patterns, lettering and seasonal borders and corners, plus instructions and suggestions for backgrounds and for putting the bulletin boards together. These four pages contain hints, tips and how-to's for using the materials in this book (and the other three books in this series) to create beautiful bulletin boards!

Backgrounds

Backgrounds are vital to the overall design of the bulletin board. In this book, simple suggestions are given for backgrounds for each bulletin board. Feel free to also experiment with materials you have on hand or which are readily available, such as:
- Textured fabrics: flannel, felt, burlap, cottons, cheesecloth
- Construction paper
- Crepe paper
- Wrapping paper, either solid color or with small print or design
- Colored tissue papers
- Newspapers
- Aluminum foil or foil-covered wrapping paper
- Brown paper bags crumpled and then flattened
- Bamboo or grass place mats or floor mats
- Colorful corrugated paper available from school supply stores
- Butcher paper
- Poster board on which figures can be permanently attached
- Maps
- Adhesive-backed plastic in a variety of colors or patterns

You may wish to choose one background which you can use for several bulletin boards during the season.

Borders

Borders make the bulletin board, so after your background is in place, it's time to frame your bulletin board with an attractive, colorful border. Three seasonal borders and matching corners are provided on pages 62 and 63 of this book for use with selected bulletin boards in this book. Other simple border suggestions are given with the remaining bulletin boards in this book.

To use the seasonal borders and corners on pages 62 and 63, duplicate enough copies of the border strip to frame the entire bulletin board. Also make four copies of the matching corner. (Corners can also be used by themselves, or with strips of construction paper forming the border.)

You may duplicate the border and corner on white paper and have the children color the border with markers. (Markers give brighter colors than crayons, so are preferable for all bulletin board work), or you may wish to reproduce the border and corner onto colored paper. (See "Duplicating Patterns and Lettering" below.)

Overlap the border strips slightly and glue or tape the sections together. Use double faced tape to attach the border and corners directly to the frame of the bulletin board or staple the border and corners to the edge of the bulletin board just inside the frame. Roll the border to store for future use.

Attractive borders can also be made with the following materials attached to the frame of the bulletin board:

- Artificial flowers, real or artificial leaves, nature items
- Rope or twine
- Braided yarn
- Wide gift-wrap ribbon
- Purchased corrugated borders available from school supply stores
- Strips of twisted crepe paper 3/4 inch wide
- Strips of construction paper cut in attractive shapes, such as scallops, zig-zags, fringes, etc.

Making Bulletin Boards Three-Dimensional

Although bulletin boards are normally flat, there are many imaginative ways you can add a three-dimensional effect to your bulletin boards. Many of the bulletin boards in this book already include ideas for three-dimensional effects, but here are more you may like to try:

- Put a cork, thick piece of cardboard, or styrofoam behind figures or lettering
- Attach large figures to the bulletin board by curving them slightly outward from the board
- Glue or attach three-dimensional or textured objects such as cotton balls, small pieces of wood, twigs, nature items, feathers, yarn, children's toys, small clothing objects (like scarves and mittens), balloons, artificial flowers or leaves, chenille wire, fabrics and burlap, bamboo or woven place mats, corrugated paper, sandpaper, crumpled aluminum foil or grocery bags, rope, drinking straws, and such
- Use artificial spray snow for a winter scene
- "Stuff" figures by putting crumpled newspaper or paper towels behind the figures before attaching to the bulletin board
- Flowers can be made from individual sections cut from egg cartons
- Heavy objects (such as a small tree branch or a toy) may be mounted securely in the following way: Cut two or more strips of bias binding tape or ribbon (available from fabric stories). Securely staple one end of the bias tape to the bulletin board, place around the item to be mounted and staple the other end (above the object) to the bulletin board so the object hangs securely on the bias tape straps.

Lettering

Each bulletin board in this book includes full-sized lettering which is to be used with the full-size patterns to create your bulletin board. To use the lettering, you may do the following:

- Cut the lettering out of any paper. Place the page(s) of lettering from this book over the sheet(s) of paper out of which you want to cut the letters. Cut through both sheets, using scissors or a craft knife. Mount letters individually on the bulletin board.
- Duplicate the lettering onto white paper and color in the letters with markers.
- Duplicate the lettering onto white or colored construction paper or copy machine paper. Cut the words apart and mount each word on the bulletin board in strip form.
- Trace the lettering onto paper of any color using colored markers. Cut out individual letters or cut apart words and use in strip form.
- Cut individual letters out of two colors of paper at once. When mounting letters on the bulletin board, lay one color on top of the other and offset the bottom letter slightly so it creates a shadow effect.

Attractive lettering can also be made by cutting letters out of wallpaper, fabrics, felt, adhesive-backed plastic in various colors or patterns, wrapping paper, grocery bags which have been crumpled and then flattened, old newspapers and other materials. For a professional look, outline letters with a dark marker for a neat edge and good contrast. Always try to use dark colors for lettering.

Textures can be used for lettering also, either by cutting the letters out of textured materials or by gluing on glitter, sequins, straw, twigs, yarn, rope, lace, craft or ice cream sticks, chenille wire or other materials.

To mount letters flat, staple to the board, use double-sided tape or roll a small piece of tape to make it double-sided. Always put the tape under the letter so it does not show.

Position letters either in a straight line or in a curved or staggered arrangement. Space letters attractively.

Duplicating Patterns and Lettering

All patterns, lettering, borders and corners in this book may be used right out of the book or traced, enlarged, reduced, duplicated or photocopied to make attractive classroom bulletin boards.

The easiest way to duplicate the materials in this book is to use a copy machine to simply copy the patterns, lettering or borders onto white or colored copy machine paper. (Copy machine paper is available in a wide variety of colors ranging from pastel colors to very bright colors.) For a very nominal price you can copy onto these colored papers at most copy centers. Construction paper also works in some copy machines.

You can also trace materials in this book onto white or colored paper by holding the page you wish to trace up to a window or by using carbon paper.

You can also color the materials from this book with markers.

The easiest way to reduce or enlarge materials is to use a copy machine which enlarges or reduces, available at most copy centers.

You can also trace the items you wish to enlarge onto a overhead projector transparency, project the transparency onto a sheet of paper on a wall, adjusting the image to the size you wish, and trace the image onto the white or colored paper. An opaque projector can also be used to enlarge patterns without having to trace them onto transparency material.

Mounting Materials on Your Bulletin Board

It is important that all materials stay securely on your bulletin board until you wish to take them down. Stapling materials directly to the bulletin board is the most secure method of mounting most materials and the staples are virtually unnoticeable. Be sure to have a staple puller handy to help prevent frustration and broken fingernails. Staples are also much better for bulletin boards for small children as it is quite difficult to pull a staple out of the bulletin boards, unlike pins and tacks. Be sure no loose staples are left on the floor after you finish putting up the bulletin board.

Pins can be used if you wish to support the materials rather than make holes. Double-faced tape, or tape rolled to make it double faced is also effective. For heavier materials, use carpet tape or packing tape.

How to Make Your Bulletin Boards Durable and Reusable

Cover both sides of your bulletin board figures with clear adhesive-backed plastic. Cut around the figures, leaving a 1/4 inch edge of plastic. (If one figure is made up of several parts, put the parts together before covering with the plastic.) You can also glue figures to colored construction paper and cut around the figure, leaving a narrow border of construction paper.

Teaching with the Bulletin Boards

Each of the bulletin boards in this book includes a suggested Bible Memory Verse and teaching tips to help you use the bulletin boards to teach important biblical concepts to your students.

In addition, children 8 years and older enjoy helping with the construction of the bulletin boards and are delighted to help cut, color, glue and staple. This provides a great opportunity for the message of the board to "soak in" while the children and teacher get to know each other better as they work together. The more the children are involved in constructing the bulletin boards, the better and more effective their learning will be.

Let's Go to Church Camp!

BIBLE CAMP
June 16-25

Appropriate for ages 7 to 12

Background and Border:

Cover bulletin board with light blue paper or burlap. Duplicate the Sunshine border and corner from pages 62 and 63 onto colored paper, or onto white paper and color with markers.

Materials and Instructions:

Duplicate the bus from pages 12 and 13 onto yellow paper or poster board, or onto poster board the color of your church bus. Cut out along heavy lines. On front of bus, cut just inside the broken line. Glue over the tab on the back of the bus, overlapping the cut edge of the front of the bus slightly over the broken line on the back of bus.

Duplicate two bus tires from page 14 and glue to bus. Using a craft knife, cut out windows of the bus. Glue black paper behind the windows.

Duplicate several children's faces from page 14. Color in facial features and clothing and glue on yarn for hair, if desired. Glue in the bus windows. Cut a curved strip of construction paper to repre-

sent a banner and letter on dates, location and details about your camp. Glue to bus.

Duplicate boy and girl figures from page 14. Color and glue on yarn for hair and clothing cut from fabrics, if desired. Mount bus on bulletin board. Staple boy and girl figures in foreground.

Cut the lettering from page 11 out of purple paper, or use in strip form.

Teaching with this Bulletin Board:

Use this bulletin board to promote your church's summer camp. Talk to the children about what happens at camp. Be sure to emphasize that camp is one place the children can learn about God and His Word, the Bible. Learn the Bible Memory Verse and talk about why it is important to "hide God's Word" in our hearts.

Suggested Bible Memory Verse:

"Thy word have I hid in mine heart, that I might not sin against Thee." — Psalm 119:11

Let's Go to Church!

Camp!

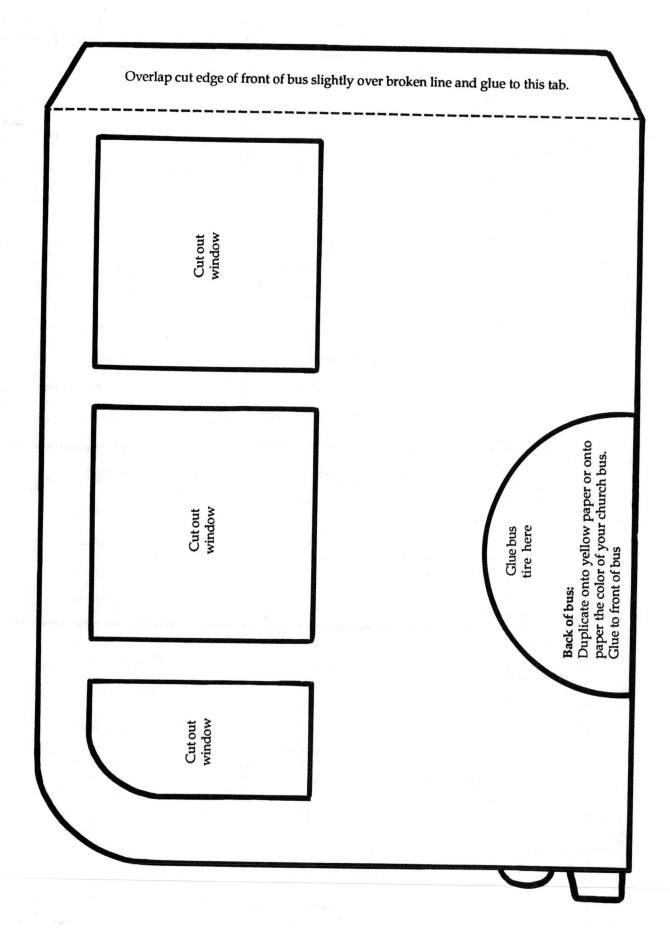

Overlap cut edge of front of bus slightly over broken line and glue to this tab.

Cut out window

Cut out window

Cut out window

Glue bus tire here

Back of bus:
Duplicate onto yellow paper or onto paper the color of your church bus.
Glue to front of bus

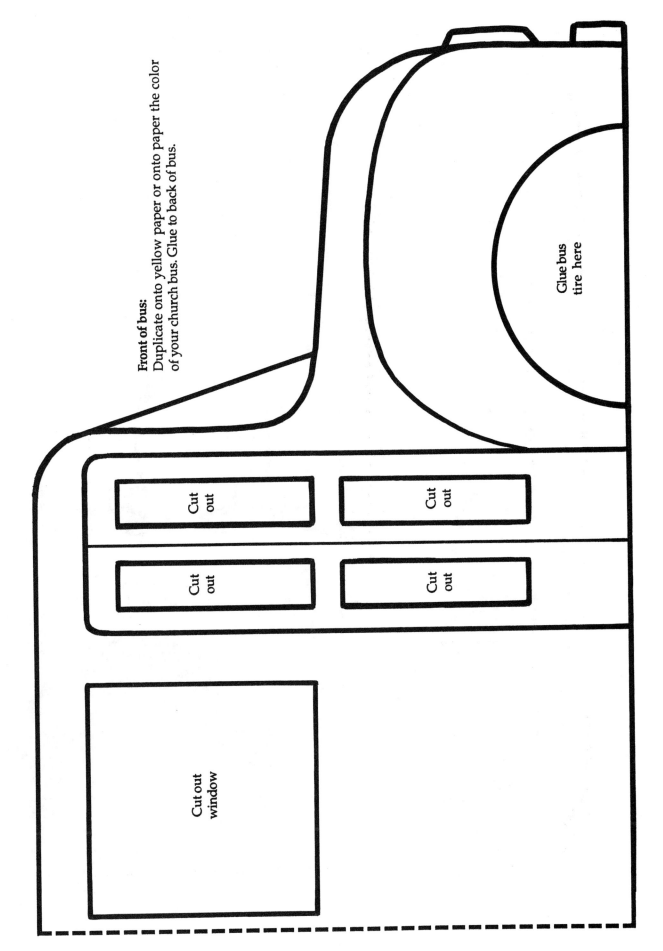

Front of bus:
Duplicate onto yellow paper or onto paper the color of your church bus. Glue to back of bus.

Glue bus
tire here

Cut
out

Cut
out

Cut
out

Cut
out

Cut out
window

Boy and girl figures:
Duplicate and color. Glue on yarn for hair and clothing cut from fabric scraps, if desired.

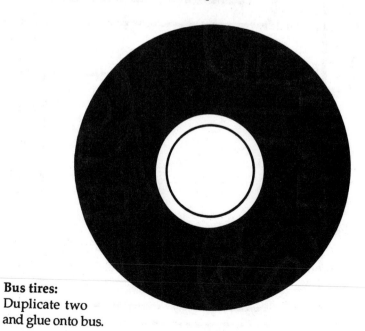

Children's faces:
Duplicate and color. Glue on yarn for hair, if desired. Glue in windows of bus.

Bus tires:
Duplicate two and glue onto bus.

14

Appropriate for ages 4 to 10

Background and Border:
Cover upper two-thirds of bulletin board with light blue paper or fabric. Cover lower one-third of bulletin board with green paper or fabric. Use red corrugated border.

Materials and Instructions:
Cut table top out of thick piece of cardboard, using illustration above as guide. Cover with red gingham fabric, allowing the edge of the fabric to hang loose along the longest edge.

For picnic table legs, cut upside-down V shapes out of cardboard and cover with wood-grain adhesive-backed plastic, or cut out of brown construction paper.

Duplicate the basket from page 17 onto tan copy machine paper or construction paper. Using a craft knife, cut along broken lines. Weave strips of brown construction paper approximately 3/4 inch wide through the slits cut in basket. Make handle from strip of tan paper.

Staple basket to bulletin board, curving it slightly for a three-dimensional effect.

Use double-sided tape to attach a small empty (and rinsed) milk carton, small empty potato chip bag (stuffed slightly with crumpled paper towels), small paper cups (glue drinking straws inside the cups first), plastic forks and/or spoons, and small empty boxes of raisins.

Duplicate lettering from page 16 onto white paper, color with red markers and mount.

Teaching with this Bulletin Board:
Learn the Bible Memory Verse. Talk about why God made Summer and some of the things that happen during Summer. Each child may pray a sentence prayer naming one thing about Summer for which he or she is thankful.

Suggested Bible Memory Verse:
"Lord, . . . You created all things." — Revelation 4:11 NIV

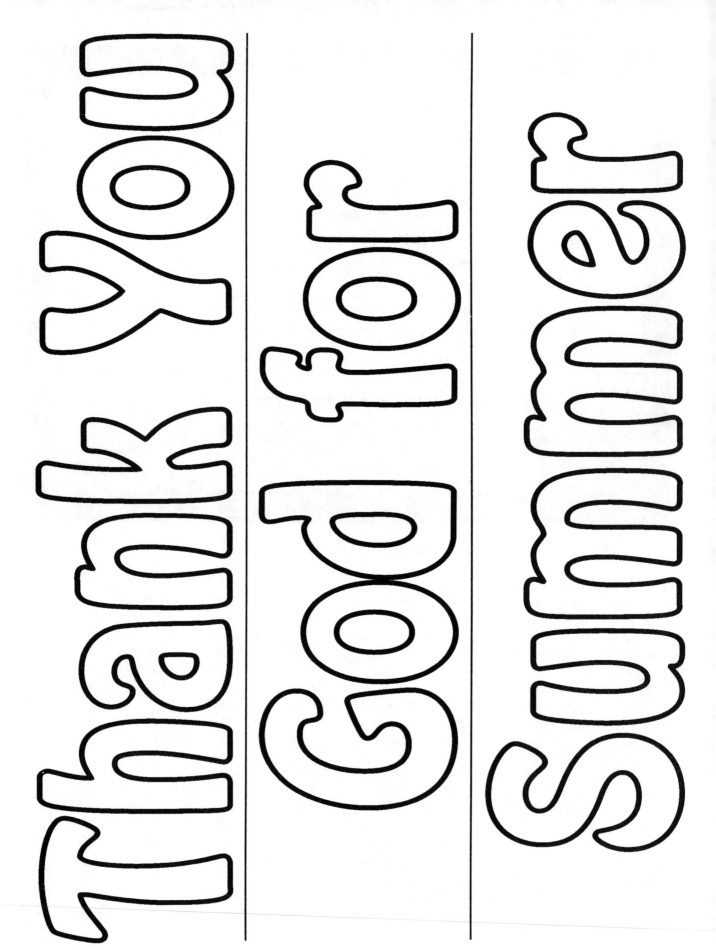

Basket pattern:
Cut on broken lines. Weave in strips of brown paper.

Appropriate for ages 9 to 12

Background and Border:
Cover bulletin board with white butcher paper. Duplicate the Summer Flowers border and corner from pages 62 and 63 onto white paper and color with markers.

Materials and Instructions:
Using the patterns on page 20, trace and cut nine flowers out of very colorful construction paper or poster board. Glue centers cut from contrasting paper onto the daisies. On each flower write one of the fruits of the Spirit from Galatians 5:22.

Form leaves and a stem for each flower out of green chenille wire and tape to the back at the bottom of each flower. Staple or tape flowers to bulletin board.

Duplicate the watering can from page 21 onto red poster board. Glue on thin strips of aluminum foil for bands and handles. Staple or tape watering can to bulletin board as shown above.

Cut lettering from page 19 out of bright red construction paper or duplicate lettering onto colored paper and use in strip form. Mount on board.

Teaching with this Bulletin Board:
Talk with the children about the fruit of the Spirit and how to dedicate their lives to the Lord completely. Discuss each fruit individually as the children may not know the meaning of each fruit. Help the children understand that to "water" means to nurture and as Christians we must try to nurture the fruit of the Spirit in our lives.

Give one flower to each of nine children. As you say the Bible Memory Verse together, have each child put the appropriate flower on the bulletin board with a pin. (Flowers can be stapled in place later.)

Suggested Bible Memory Verse:
"The fruit of the Spirit is love, joy, peace, patience, kindness, goodness, faithfulness, gentleness and self-control." — Galatians 5:22 NIV

Water These Flowers

Flowers:
Cut out patterns and use to trace nine colorful flowers.

Watering Can:
Duplicate onto red poster board. Glue on narrow
strips of aluminum foil for bands and handles.

Appropriate for ages 7 to 11

Background and Border:

Use tan or light brown fabric or paper for background. Fringe strips of green construction paper to simulate grass; staple along the bottom. Cut scalloped green borders for top and sides.

Materials and Instructions:

Staple small dessert-size paper plates to the board, overlapping slightly, to form the body of the caterpillar. Use one plate for each student; leave extra plates for additional or new children. Draw the caterpillar's face on a plate.

Out of black construction paper, cut one foot, duplicated from the pattern on page 23, for each paper plate and staple to board. Duplicate the caterpillar's hat from page 23 onto gold construction paper and cut out. Staple in place. (You could use a child-sized straw hat instead.)

Make butterflies by cutting bodies out of colorful tissue paper using pattern on page 23. Put together in layers and form the butterflies bodies

and antennae with chenille wire. Staple or glue butterflies randomly on board.

Mount a picture of each student in the center of each plate and write the child's name below the picture. The children may add stickers or gold stars for specific achievements.

Cut lettering from pages 24 and 25 out of brown or rust construction paper, or duplicate onto complimentary-color paper and use in strip form.

Teaching with this Bulletin Board:

Learn the Bible Memory Verse together. Discuss ways in which the children can work together in cooperation to achieve a group goal. If desired, choose a class project; a specific task could be assigned to each child and written under the child's name and picture on the paper plate.

Suggested Bible Memory Verse:

"Being fruitful in every good work, and increasing in the knowledge of God." — Colossians 1:10

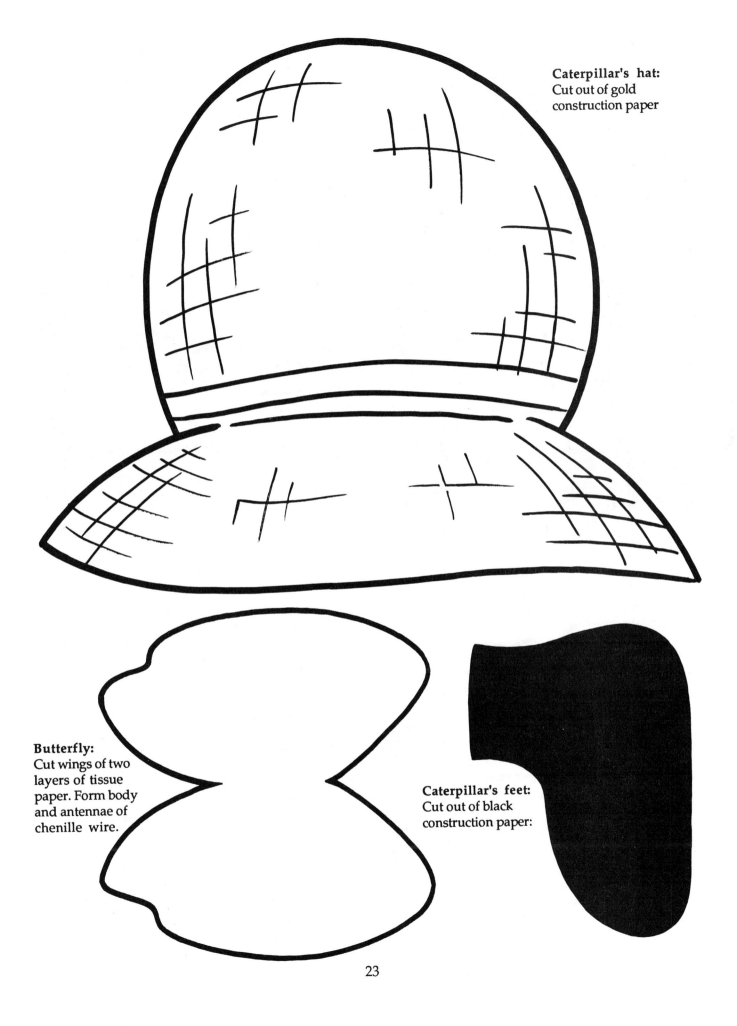

Caterpillar's hat:
Cut out of gold
construction paper

Butterfly:
Cut wings of two
layers of tissue
paper. Form body
and antennae of
chenille wire.

Caterpillar's feet:
Cut out of black
construction paper:

23

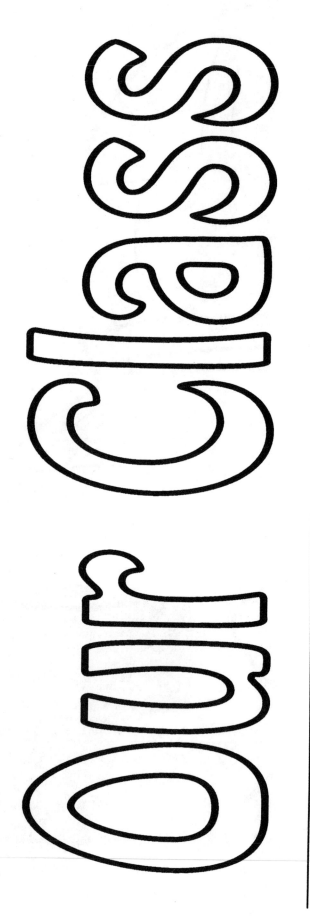

Our Class

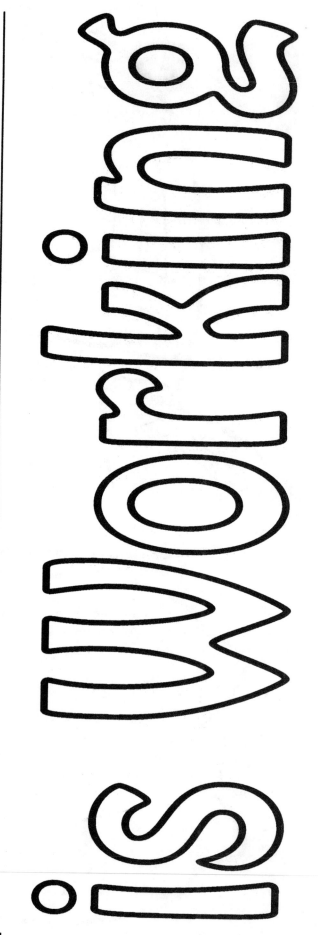

is Working!

Together

For Jesus

Appropriate for ages 8 to 11

Background and Border:

Cover bulletin board with light yellow paper or fabric. Duplicate Summer Flowers border and corner from pages 62 and 63 onto white paper and color with markers.

Materials and Instructions:

Cut a large mushroom out of a grocery bag which has been crumpled and then flattened. Before stapling the mushroom to the bulletin board, "stuff" it slightly with crumpled newspapers or paper towels to give it a slight three-dimensional effect.

Duplicate the frog and frog legs from pages 29 and 30 onto green construction paper or poster board. (If desired, the frog's body could be a slightly lighter green than the legs.) Glue on large movable eyes.

Glue the legs onto the frog, overlapping the body over the legs up to the broken line on the legs. Allow glue to dry, then staple frog in place on top of mushroom on bulletin board.

Cut lettering from pages 27 and 28 out of dark brown construction paper or felt, or duplicate the lettering onto tan paper and use in strip form.

Teaching with this Bulletin Board:

Ask the children to tell what it means to know Jesus. Explain the plan of salvation. Tell the children that when they accept Jesus as their Savior, they will know Jesus and the "power of His resurrection." Be sure to also mention that once they have accepted Jesus as Savior, Jesus wants us to study the Bible, go to church and learn about Him so we can know Him better, just like we get to know a new friend better when we spend time with them. Learn the Bible Memory Verse together.

Suggested Bible Memory Verse:

"I want to know Christ and the power of His resurrection." — Philippians 3:10 NIV

TO

HOP

IT!

LET'S

Get To Know Jesus!

Frog's body:
Duplicate onto green
construction paper or poster
board. Overlap body over legs
up to broken line and glue.

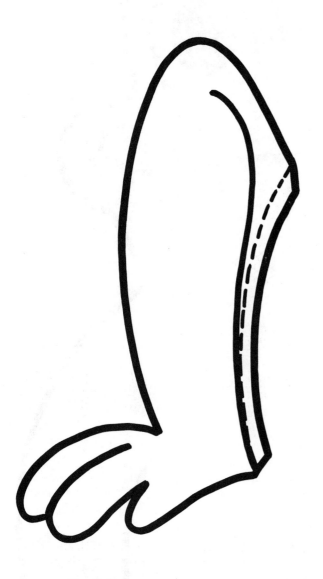

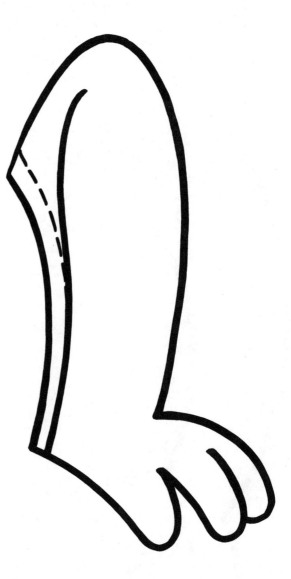

Frog's legs:
Duplicate onto green construction paper or poster board. Glue legs to body, with body overlapping up to broken line.

Appropriate for ages 8 to 12

Background and Border:

Cover bulletin board with yellow paper, fabric or burlap. Cut strips of green construction paper for border on the top and two sides. For bottom, cut wider strips of green construction paper to represent grass as shown above.

Materials and Instructions:

Cut two trees out of brown poster board, construction paper or grocery bags which have been crumpled and then flattened. Cut leafy part of trees out of green construction paper. Staple trees to bulletin board.

Construct a hammock for the lion out of nylon net or a net bag in which fruits and vegetables are sold. Use lightweight rope to tie the hammock between the trees.

Duplicate lion and lion's tail from pages 32 and 33 onto gold or yellow construction paper or poster board. Glue on black felt nose and eyes. Glue gold or yellow yarn on mane and tip of tail.

Place lion into hammock. Staple lion to hammock so lion does not slide down into hammock. Attach lion's tail to lion where marked so the tail hangs outside the hammock.

Cut the lettering from pages 34 and 35 out of dark green construction paper or poster board, or duplicate lettering onto colored paper and use in strip form.

Teaching with this Bulletin Board:

Help the children name reasons we should attend Sunday school each week and not yield to the temptation to sleep late or have our own fun or play when we should be at church. Help them think of the important things we learn at church. Then learn the Bible Memory Verse. What should we love about God's house?

Suggested Bible Memory Verse:

"Lord, I have loved. . .Your house." — Psalm 26:8 NKJV

ATTACH
TAIL
HERE

Lion:
Duplicate onto gold or yellow construction paper or poster board. Glue yellow or gold yarn on mane and glue on black felt eyes and nose.

Lion's tail:
Duplicate onto gold or yellow
construction paper or poster board.
Glue on yellow or gold yarn.

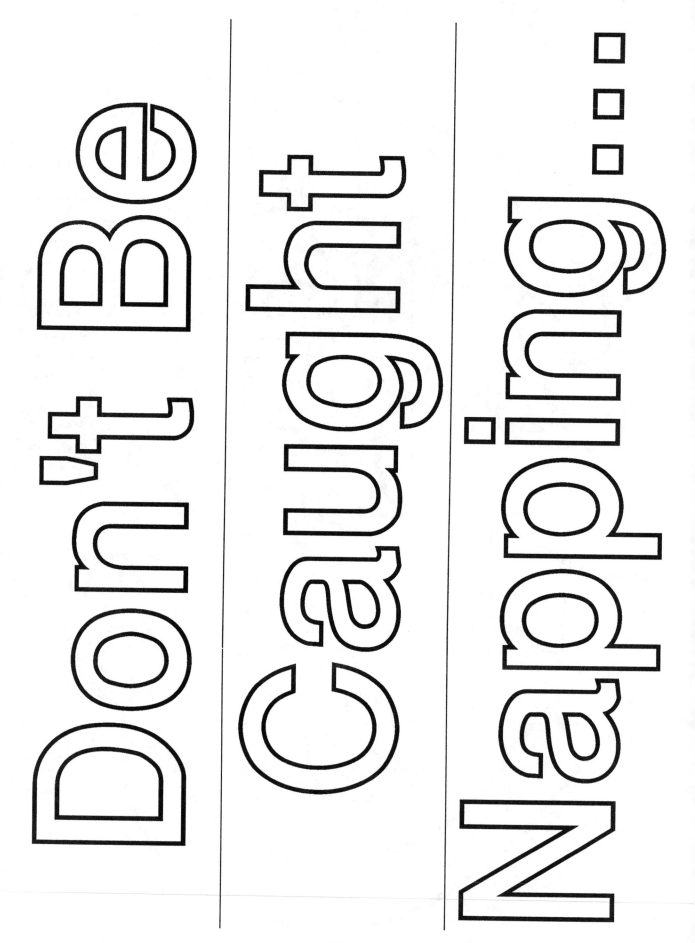

Don't Be
Caught
Napping...

Come To Sunday School!

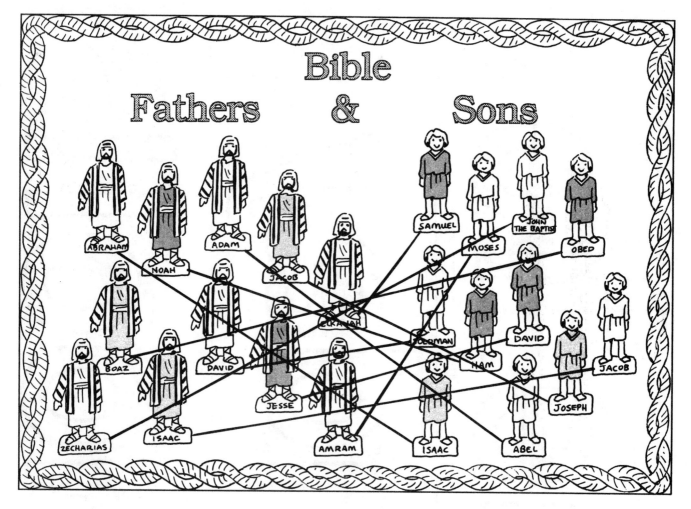

Bible Fathers & Sons

Appropriate for ages 9 to 12

Background and Border:

Cover the board with tan burlap. Border is made of strands of rope or yarn in natural colors.

Materials and Instructions:

Duplicate the father and the child from page 38 11 times. On the base of each figure write a name from the proper category below. Tape a long piece of yarn to the back of each father.

Randomly arrange fathers on one side of the board and sons on the other. Let the yarn hang down. Place a push pin near each child.

Duplicate lettering from page 37 onto golden-rod paper and mount on bulletin board.

Teaching with this Bulletin Board:

Briefly tell (or review) the story of each father on the board with the children. The child who guesses correctly who the father's son was may string the piece of yarn attached to the father over to the push pin near the son. Repeat until all fathers and sons are matched up. (The yarns may be re-leased from the pins so children can match up the fathers and sons again.)

Emphasize good and bad behaviors. Discuss how children should act toward their parents. Learn the Bible Memory Verse.

Correct matches of fathers and sons:

Abraham	Isaac
Noah	Ham
Adam	Abel
Jacob	Joseph
David	Solomon
Isaac	Jacob
Jesse	David
Zecharias	John the Baptist
Amram	Moses
Boaz	Obed
Elkanah	Samuel

Suggested Bible Memory Verse:

"Children, obey your parents in the Lord: for this is right." — Ephesians 6:1

Bible

Fathers

& Sons

Bible-times father:
Duplicate 11 onto various colors of paper, or duplicate onto white paper, color in and glue on clothing cut from fabric.

Bible-times child:
Duplicate 11 onto various colors of paper, or duplicate onto white paper, color in and glue on clothing cut from fabric.

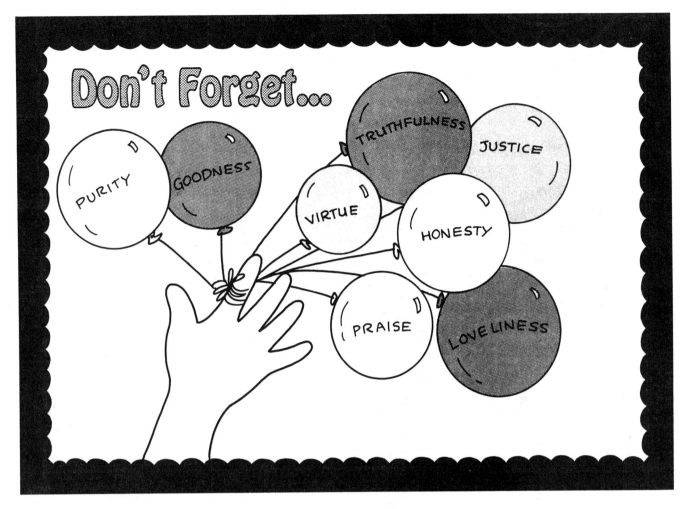

Appropriate for ages 9 to 12

Background and Border:

Cover bulletin board with light blue paper or fabric. Use yellow corrugated border or cut construction paper strips in scalloped shapes.

Materials and Instructions:

Cut out hand pattern from page 41. Trace around it onto paper or poster board. Mount in lower left corner of bulletin board.

Cut eight large balloons out of various bright colors of construction paper or wrapping paper with a small design. Tape a long piece of string or yarn to the back of each balloon. On each balloon write one of the things we are to think about from Philippians 4:8 as shown above. Mount the balloons in a pleasing arrangement on the bulletin board. Bring all the balloon strings together and tie around one finger of the hand.

(Real balloons can also be used. Inflate, but do not use helium. Use double-sided tape to attach balloons to the bulletin board. Carefully write on the balloons with a broad-tip marker.)

Duplicate lettering from page 40 onto dark blue paper and cut out individual letters. Glue on a light coating of glitter before mounting

Teaching with this Bulletin Board:

Say the Bible Memory Verse to the children slowly. Discuss each of the things Paul says we are to think about as the children may not know the meaning of all. Talk about ways we can live each of these things in our daily lives.

As you learn the verse, let children point to the correct word on the bulletin board.

(Children could make miniature pictures to take home to help them remember the verse.)

Suggested Bible Memory Verse:

"Finally, brethren, whatsoever things are true, whatsoever things are honest, whatsoever things are just, whatsoever things are pure, whatsoever things are lovely, whatsoever things are of good report; if there be any virtue, and if there be any praise, think on these things." — Philippians 4:8

Don't

Forget...

Hand pattern:
Trace onto construction paper or poster board and cut out.

Appropriate for ages 4 to 12

Background and Border:

Cover bulletin board with light yellow fabric, paper or burlap. Twist narrow strips of orange and green crepe paper one inch wide together and tape to bulletin board frame. Loop another crepe paper streamer across top of bulletin board as shown. Attach balloons in upper corners also.

Materials and Instructions:

Duplicate four or more boy and girl figures from pages 44 and 45. Color in skin tones, clothing and hair. (Clothing can also be cut out of fabric scraps and glued on.)

Cut triangular-shaped flags for each child to carry out of brightly colored construction paper. Cut one flag significantly larger than the rest. Glue a piece of chenille wire to each flag to form the flag's pole. Glue other end of chenille wire onto boy and girl figures. Allow to dry. Carefully write on each flag one aspect of VBS which you wish to promote such as songs, Bible stories, games, crafts, snacks, puppets, etc. On the large flag, write the place,

dates, time and other details concerning your specific VBS.

Staple boy and girl figures and flags to the bulletin board. If desired, bend chenille wire slightly so flags stick out from the board.

Cut lettering from page 43 out of dark green construction paper or use in strip form.

Teaching with this Bulletin Board:

Put this bulletin board up the first week you wish to promote VBS. Talk with the children about what VBS is and what will happen at VBS. Have children who have attended before tell what happens and how much fun they had. Then learn the Bible Memory Verse. Encourage children to bring their friends.

(You may wish to send notes home to the parents telling about VBS.)

Suggested Bible Memory Verse:

"I was glad when they said unto me, Let us go into the house of the Lord." — Psalm 122:1

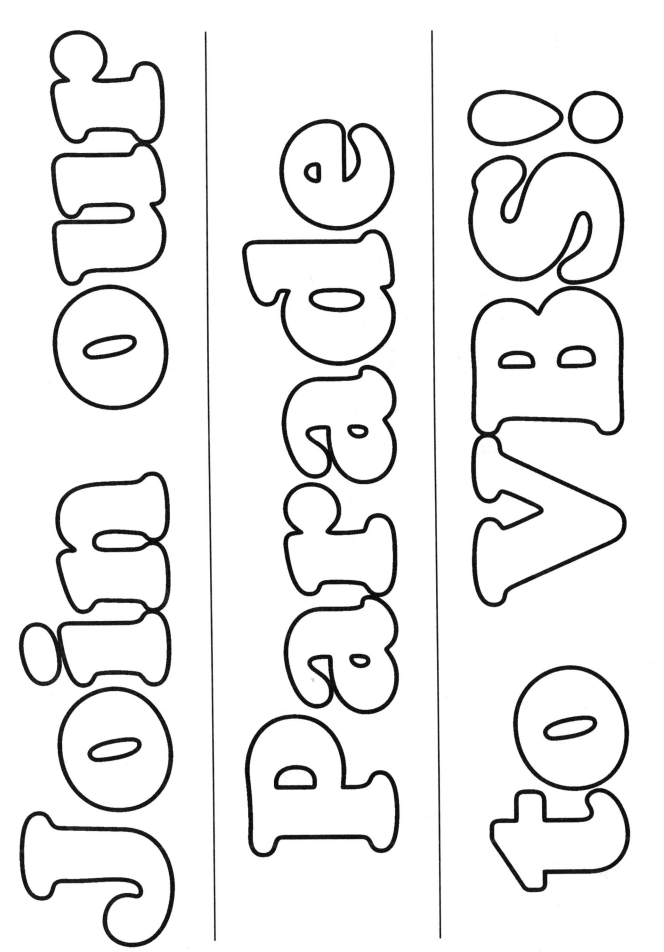

Join Our Parade to VBS!

Girl:
Duplicate and cut out. Color in skin tones and clothing. Or cut clothing out of fabric scraps and glue on.

Boy:
Duplicate and cut out. Color in skin tones and clothing. Or cut clothing out of fabric scraps and glue on.

Appropriate for ages 9 to 12

Background and Border:

Cover bulletin board with blue paper or fabric. Duplicate the Summertime Celebration border and corner from pages 62 and 63 onto white paper and color with red and blue markers.

Materials and Instructions:

Duplicate the bell and star from pages 48 and 49 onto white copy machine paper or construction paper and cut out. Glue knocker cut from gold-colored paper or aluminum foil on bell. Cut several additional stars out of red and/or gold construction paper. Glue one red or gold star behind one white star, shifting the red or gold star so it creates a shadow effect. Allow glue to dry.

Duplicate the lettering from page 47 onto bright gold paper and cut out. Outline with a black or blue marker.

Teaching with this Bulletin Board:

Give each child a star or bell. As you talk about the freedoms we enjoy, let the children write a freedom on each bell and star. The children may decorate their bells and stars with colorful foil star stickers, if desired, and then pin their bells and stars on the bulletin board. (They can be stapled in position later.)

Discuss and learn the Bible Memory Verse together. Emphasize to the children that it is important for us to fear (serve) the Lord so that He will continue to bless our nation as He has done. Lead the children in prayer to thank God for our nation and to ask Him to continue to bless it.

Suggested Bible Memory Verse:

"Surely His salvation is near to those who fear Him, That glory may dwell in our land." — Psalm 85:9 NKJV

Let Freedom Ring!

We have freedom to

Star:
Duplicate several onto white paper. Cut the same
number out of red and/or gold paper and glue behind
white stars for shadow effect.

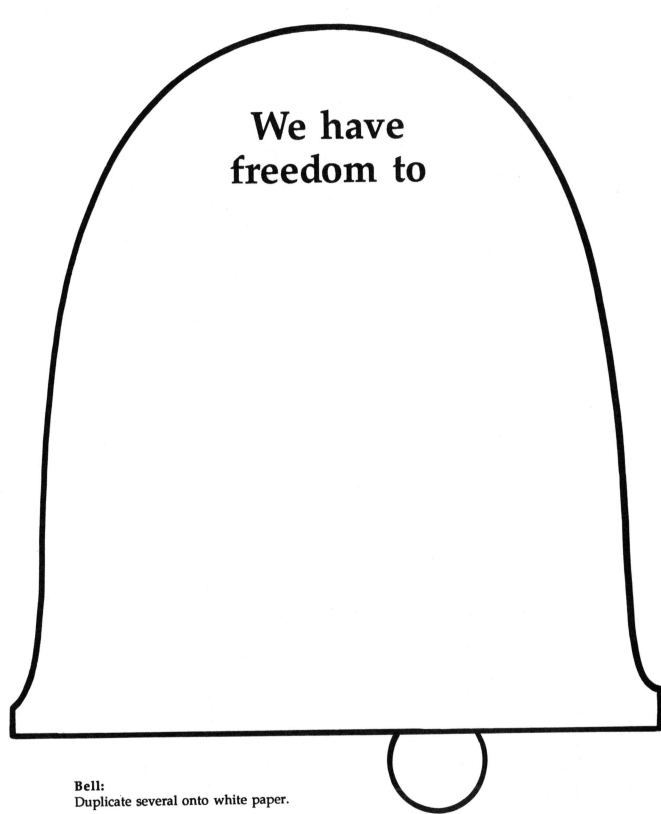

We have freedom to

Bell:
Duplicate several onto white paper.

Appropriate for ages 7 to 11

Background and Border:

Cover the bulletin board with light blue paper or fabric. Use yellow corrugated border or cut scalloped strips of construction paper or wrapping paper.

Materials and Instructions:

Find two small tree branches similar in size and shape. Fasten to the bulletin board using bias tape strips. (See page 7.) Cut free-form shapes of green construction paper and glue or tape to the top of the tree branches to represent leafy areas.

Tie a piece of lightweight rope or twine between the tree branches.

Cut out the patterns for the dress and shirt from page 51. Trace onto several colors of construction paper and cut out. Use real clothespins or toy-size clothespins to clip the clothing cut-outs to the clothesline.

Cut the lettering from pages 52 and 53 out of purple or dark blue paper or felt, or duplicate the lettering onto colored paper and use in strip form.

Teaching with this Bulletin Board:

Ask the children in turn to tell their plans for the summer. Then ask them to name how they will serve the Lord this summer. Discuss ways we can serve the Lord; be sure the children understand they can serve the Lord while they are playing and doing ordinary things.

Each child may write the way he or she will serve the Lord on one of the clothing cut-outs from page 51 and clip it on the clothesline. Children may decorate their clothing cut-outs with crayons, markers or stickers, if desired. Learn the Bible Memory Verse together.

Suggested Bible Memory Verse:

"Serve the Lord with gladness: come before His presence with singing." — Psalm 100:2

Patterns for dress and shirt:
Trace and cut out several from various
colors of construction paper.

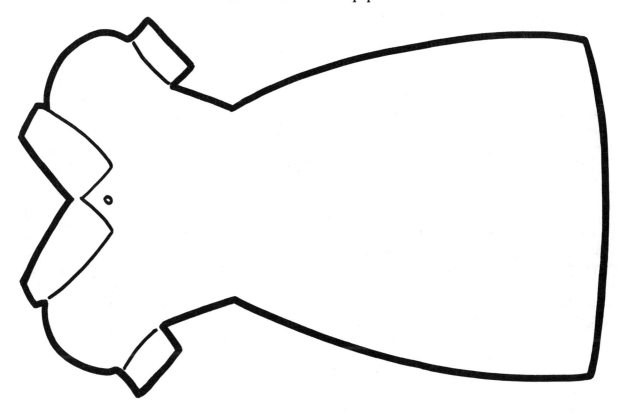

Line up

Ways to

Serve

Jesus

This

Summer

Appropriate for ages 9 to 12

Background and Border:

Cover bulletin board with silver wrapping paper. Use strips of gold wrapping paper, cut into zig-zag shapes, for the border.

Materials and Instructions:

Trace the sun's mouth, nose and eyes from page 55 onto bright yellow poster board using a black marker. Cut out along heavy outside lines. Also cut out 18 triangular sunbursts using the pattern on page 55. If desired, glue large movable eyes onto the eyes cut from yellow poster board.

Carefully position all 18 triangular sunbursts into a circle on the bulletin board. (Cut a circle about seven inches in diameter out of newspaper as a guide. Use double-sided tape on the back of each sunburst.)

After sunbursts are in position, add the eyes, nose and mouth, using double-faced tape on the back of each.

Cut lettering from pages 56 and 57 out of dark blue construction paper or poster board, or duplicate lettering onto brightly colored copy machine paper and use in strip form.

Teaching with this Bulletin Board:

Ask the children to name ways they can "spread sunshine" and help to make others happy. Talk about the joy which the Lord gives and how they can share that joy with others. (If there are children who have not accepted Jesus as their Savior, present the plan of salvation and if they wish, help them to accept Jesus now so they can experience the joy of the Lord also.) Learn the Bible Memory Verse together. Each child could name one reason he or she is glad in the Lord today.

Suggested Bible Memory Verse:

"Be glad in the Lord." — Psalm 32:11

Sun's face:
Trace onto bright yellow poster board using à black marker.

Sunbursts:
Cut 18 out of bright
yellow poster board.

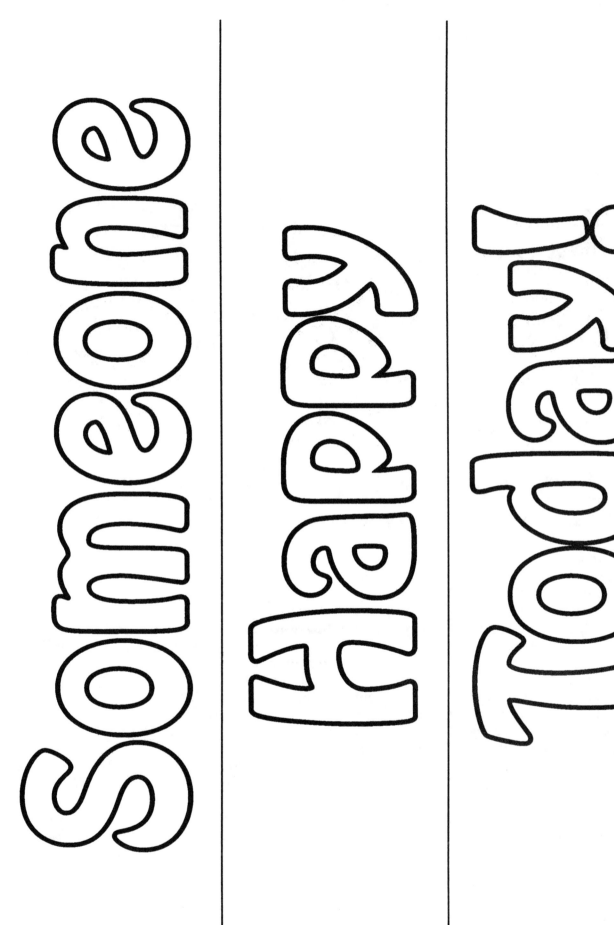

Someone

Happy

Today!

Appropriate for ages 7 to 12

Background and Border:

This bulletin board helps teach children the plan of salvation from God's Word.

Cover the bulletin board with light blue paper or fabric. Duplicate the Summer Flowers border and corner from pages 62 and 63.

Materials and Instructions:

Using the pattern on page 60, cut six stems out of green construction paper and write the number and Scripture reference for one of the verses on each. Cut six flowers from page 60. Glue one flower to the top of each stem.

Cut lettering out of gold paper.

Teaching with this Bulletin Board:

Give each child a bee duplicated from page 60. Place all near the first flower.

Talk about the meaning of each verse and invite the children to accept Jesus as Savior. Each week, talk about the next verse and help children learn it. When a child learns a verse, he moves his bee to that flower.

Present the certificate on page 61 to each child who learns the verses.

Suggested Bible Memory Verse:

1. *"There is none righteous, no, not one."* — Romans 3:10

2. *"For all have sinned, and come short of the glory of God."* — Romans 3:23

3. *"For the wages of sin is death; but the gift of God is eternal life through Jesus Christ our Lord."* — Romans 6:23

4. *"But God commendeth His love toward us, in that, while we were yet sinners, Christ died for us."* — Romans 5:8

5. *"If thou shalt confess with thy mouth the Lord Jesus, and shalt believe in thine heart that God hath raised Him from the dead, thou shalt be saved."* — Romans 10:9

6. *"If we confess our sins, He is faithful and just to forgive us our sins, and to cleanse us from all unrighteousness."* — I John 1:9

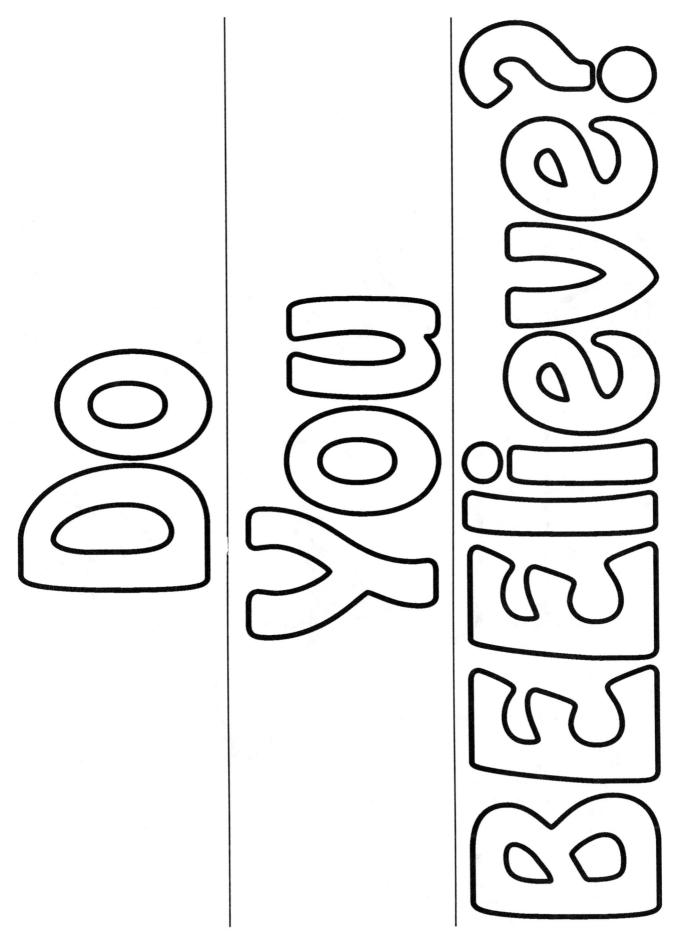

Do you Believe?

Flower:
Cut six out of various colors of
construction paper. Glue
to top of flower stem.

Flower stem:
Cut six out of green construction paper.
Write number and reference of a
Bible Memory Verse on each stem.

Bee:
Duplicate one bee for each child.
Children are to put their name on the bee.
They may color the bee if desired.

In recognition of outstanding
efforts and accomplishments,
this CERTIFICATE of AWARD
is presented to

for:

Date

Signature

Sunshine Corner

Summertime Celebration Corner

Summer Flowers Corner

How to Use Summer
Borders and Corners

Choose the border you wish to use. Duplicate enough copies of that border strip to cover the entire frame of your bulletin board. In addition, make four copies of the matching corner.

You may duplicate the borders and corners onto white paper and color in the borders with markers. (The children will enjoy helping you do this.)

Or you may wish to duplicate the borders and corners onto colored copy machine paper or construction paper which compliments the background colors in the bulletin board.

Overlap the border strips slightly and glue or tape the sections together. Roll the border to store for future use.

Sunshine Border　　　　**Summertime Celebration Border**　　　　**Summer Flowers Border**

63